Wonderment...

for Elinor

Contents

Hello. 7

Part I 9

An Ode to Wimbledon 10

I'm Worried About that E-mail I just Sent Because 12

I Didn't Get a Reply 12

I Went to the Doctor Because the Voices Told Me To 13

Old Lady at the End of the Pier What's Your Story? 14

My Gay T-Shirt 17

The Sweetest Thing 18

The Low Poem 19

Don't Start What You Can't Finish 20

Old Man Taking a Bath 21

Rocket Launcher Xmas 22

It's 2am 24

A Warm Story 25

The Taste of Carpet 28

Insecurity 29

Part II 31

True Story 33

Cardiff Bay Hates Rollerbladers 34

Hug Goodbye 36

The Breakup 37

Every Six Seconds 38

Mariana's Trench 39

The Master Storyteller 40
Everyone Has at Least One Book in Them 42
It Could Happen to You 43
The Castle 44
Five Days Left to Live 48
Goodbye.. 50
About the Author 52

Hello.

You're amazing. Go on, stand up and say it. 'I'm amazing'. Shout it from the rooftops, jump out of the bath and run down the street saying it, write a letter to your nearest relative asking them to repeat it a thousand times in the Ra language of the Tibetan highlands to a bandashi goat while rutting a sandwich maker over and over again until they promise you free egg and cress bagels for life.

You see, life's hard. There's war, there's a boss that should be in a circus, there's stolen yellow sunglasses with a tint of anger, there's tablets for nakedness, there's scribbled notes in the dead of the night that speak of money thoughts, there's fun vegetables that fail their courses, there's keys for light-bulbs, there's a herb garden of fresh toothaches, there's racist nipple hairs, there's borders of rhythm and cores of Reality TV, there's gaps where there's words and words where there's a WiFi link, there's a man shouting *right now* that his arm fell out due to a leprous wizard, there's a bunch of flowers sitting behind the laughter, there's eight bottles of champagne in an empty box, there's a pair of ski socks that you wear to prevent your feet from exploding, there's a clock ticking down to the end of your life and there's not enough time to follow the yellow brick road to your dreams while the bulldozer of time pushes you towards your grave. Look – behind you, there's a strip of lights crying under your partner who is sharpening a blade to bury in your back while you cook a meal of lettuce and despair. Life's shit.

But you deserve to be happy. Others should be envious of you. Others ARE envious. I am, you sound awesome. Others should want to be with you or be you or be both at the same time. You'll inspire others. You'll do it again. And again. You won't know it. You'll be modest, you'll be arrogant, you'll be you. Brilliant and complicated. Loved and hated. It's all about you.

You're amazing. People should know.

This book is for you.

P.s. What’s your name again?

Part I

An Ode to Wimbledon

Cute ball girl out of focus on my TV screen

Cute ball girl I hope you're over sixteen

Cute ball girl when a shot is out you shout 'over-rule',

Cute ball girl I realise you're not a ball girl at all,

Cute line judge the TV turns on you again,

Cute line judge you're older than Tutankhamen.

Bearded
lady

I'm Worried About that E-mail I just Sent Because I Didn't Get a Reply

I'm worried about that e-mail I just sent because I didn't get a reply,
Were you offended about the syntax because words never lie?
Were you offended about the length, because quality counts,
But you know I've got money because you've seen my bank accounts,
Did I not put a smiley face where a joke was demanded,
Or did I put LOL which made me sound retarded.
I still want the egg whisk,
I really do,
But I don't want to blow the sale,
Because I put 'Kind Regards' instead of 'Thank you'.
I'm worried about the e-mail, I didn't get a reply,
You're the cute girl in the office and this is no lie,
I checked and I'm pretty sure it's not sexual harassment
To ask if I look good with my ass bent
Over the photocopier, but apparently it is.

I Went to the Doctor Because the Voices Told Me To

I went to the doctor because the voices told me to,

He said, 'You're hearing things, punch me in the face.' So I did.

It turns out he didn't actually say that.

Or that I should pull his trousers down and sleep with him while he was unconscious.

Old Lady at the End of the Pier What's Your Story?

Old lady at the end of the pier what's your story?
When you were young, did you teach yourself how to act,
Get your bags packed,
And head into London looking for glory?
Did you think you would meet all the stars there,
Dance with Ginger Rogers and meet Fred Astaire?
Did you start off small, and find a nice a pub,
Acting out new plays above the hubbub?
Did an agent discover you who wasn't an agent at all,
But a pimp with a suit on, playing you for a fool.
But you weren't to be fooled, oh no, you knew his game,
You got out, but too late – with an addiction to cocaine.

Did your best friend, at the pub, die of Aids,
Which upset you, and all the other barmaids,
Did your addiction get worse, until to get a fix,
You went back to the pimp and started turning tricks.
Did a real agent come along – he loved you - he'd seen you act,
But the pimp told him you're a prostitute and he tore up the contract.
Did you have no money, and no way to escape,
So you stole a baseball bat and acquired some tape.
Did you tie up that pimp and bash in his head,
Swinging over and over until he was dead.
Did that simple act not quench your rage,
And throughout London, did you go on a rampage
Of death?

Old lady at the end of the pier what's your story?

In your broken wheelchair you look so poorly,

I think you're someone's Gran, just watching the boats sail,

And not a mass murderer, recently let out of jail.

Wonderment...

My Gay T-Shirt

I know my favourite t-shirt makes me look gay,

But I'm open minded or so it seems that way,

I went to a gay club and they let me straight in,

When I answered 'Why yes, I do have a nipple ring'

I danced all night, until the break of day,

When the t-shirt came out and blew them away,

I had no idea a t-shirt could perform fellacio,

In a club with such a high male to female ratio.

I've never slept with a man, with women I flirt,

I definitely can't say the same about my favourite t-shirt.

When I washed clean it again and again,

It did no good - it still smelt of other men's semen.

My favourite t-shirt had committed no sin,

But I still threw the slag into the bin.

The Sweetest Thing

I opened the CD case of the CD I remembered from childhood,

The CD case was empty.

I opened the next CD case,

It contained the CD of the previous CD case and the CD for this case and I was happy.

The Low Poem

I'm low,

Like Christmas with no snow,

I'm low,

Like a circus without a show,

I'm low,

Like a pizza without pepperami,

A general without an army,

Like a ninja who wants to harm me,

I'm low.

Luckily there's no ninjas that want to harm me.

Which is one positive I guess...

I'm low,

Like a doughnut without any dough,

Like a rower unable to row,

Like a sewer unable to sew,

I'm low.

I shouldn't've been so slow,

In the go-kart competition,

I came last.

Don't Start What You Can't Finish

Pinch, punch it's the first of the month

A punch and a kick for being so quick

A smack and a whack for hurting me back

A jab with a knife for being older in life

A shot in the head - it's the 1st, now you're dead.

...A suicide bomb for the day being wrong

A grenade or two as the month is new

Don't ask me the date - it'll all escalate,

And make everyone irate,

And it'll seem like it's fate

That your pinch, punch before,

Has started nuclear war...

Old Man Taking a Bath

Sun, sand, sea and in the distance two mottled islands poking out of the tropical waters.

Which reminded me so strongly of something I couldn't quite put my finger on.

Rocket Launcher Xmas

Rocket launcher Christmas,
Rocket launcher Christmas,
Rocket launcher Christmas,
Must be Al-Qaeda

Rocket launcher Christmas,
Rocket launcher Christmas,
Rocket launcher Christmas,
Must be Al-Qaeda

If you get five years for owning a gun,
What to you get for a rocket launcher?
I looked it up and it turns out it's three years,
Which almost makes it worth having a rocket launcher,

Rocket launcher Christmas,
Rocket launcher Christmas,
Rocket launcher Christmas,
Must be Al-Qaeda

Rocket launcher Christmas,
I'm going to return it,
Did you keep the receipt?

I ♥ Your hair

It's 2am

It's 2am and I realise I've reached a new low point in my life as I'm on the internet watching a naked woman play chess

But then I realise there are people in Africa who can't get to the internet to watch a naked woman play chess and I cheer up

A Warm Story

Above cold air too far to fly,
I once did happen to espy,
A bird struggling 'gainst the cold,
With frozen wings that would not fold.

That bird did fall to the ground,
With more a thump than it should sound,
A glacial ball of frozen fur,
Scared to what might now occur.

A passing cow noticed not its state,
And on that bird it did defecate,
But what that cow did now excrete,
Contained an awful lot of heat.

The bird defrosted all way through,
Was warm and happy, it was true,
It began to sing out loud and gay,
When a passing cat stopped on its way.

The song was loud and easily heard,
And the cat dug in to save that bird,
It cleaned him off that saviour moggy,
Then ate him whole save that was soggy.

The story that I tell you now,
Is not 'bout bird, cat or cow,

But if you wish some rules to follow,
I will recount the story's moral.

A person who sh*ts on you when low,
Is not necessarily a foe,
And someone who's help he does then lend,
Is not necessarily a friend.

And if you're in a warm and happy place,
Don't stick your neck out, show your face,
If you're warm and happy there,
Be contented then with your fare.

We're Naked!!!

Bzzz

Danger – Do not get naked

The Taste of Carpet

I started eating carpet in my teens
It was such a small piece
With a thin pile and fluffy in its newness.
Just a curious lick.

One night in Australia, drunk,
I again wrapped my tongue around some Antipodean carpet,
But the unkept stubble of it coursed my chin and
I regretted it in the morning

More recently a neater carpet
A thin strip,
Between two round pink fleshy skirting boards
Surprisingly,
Gave me a stomach upset,

While another time,
A brown Hessian, unkempt square
That led from the front to the back of the house
Tasted of a welcome mat,
That everyone had wiped their feet on before entering.

Insecurity

Can you see my nipples through this shirt?
It's quite cold in here so they must be quite pert,
I know this is all going quite bad,
This could be the worse job interview I've ever had.

You offered me a glass of wine when I arrived,
But it doesn't matter, I've already had five,
I slurred before when I talked about my degree,
And there's a damp patch on my trousers that looks like pee.
(but it isn't...it's coffee...honestly)

I touched your bum when I came in, I'm sure you felt it,
And the garlic I had for lunch it looks like you smelt it,
But the first was a mistake – I should've moved my hand away faster,
And the second was hidden in some penne pasta.

Won't you give me a job, it'll prove to me,
I'm not a loser, crippled by insecurity.
I'll work long hours, put others to shame,
And when things go wrong I won't shirk the blame.
I'll work like ten men, I'll beat all the rest,
And when I'm finished you and your company, will be the best.

But before I go, and you say, 'He's the one, he's got it',
Don't look down, 'cos on my shoe, I think there's some dog sh...

Part II

True Story

So every day I pass in and out of the entrance and exit of the hospital lobby as a shortcut to get to the bus stop for my job as chief fryer in KFC, always saying Hi to the security guard on the desk as I pass and then one day the guard Steve stops me and says, We're upgrading the security systems here - I need to issue you with an ID he says so what's your full name, uh huh, uh huh, and what department do you work in? He says, and I say cardiology and he says I look like a cardiologist and I say I know, and I receive my ID card and I carry on to the bus stop and now I am receiving calls throughout the night and having to perform open heart surgery on pensioners and company executives.

Cardiff Bay Hates Rollerbladers

There are bumps all over the pavement,

There are random cobbles that can only be meant,

To knock you on your ass,

Street signs that tell you not to pass,

But it doesn't stop there, oh no,

There are:

People with pitchforks shouting with abandon -

A blind man with a shotgun shooting at random -

Women flashing their breasts to put you off -

Policemen making arrests – men pulling you off -

A land of dinosaurs forgotten until now –

A huge scorpion the size of a cow –

A man's intestines twelve miles long -

Wait...

I've just realised

Katie Perry was in that Gym Class Heroes song.

Those are some of the things that make you afraid,

To be the guy on the rollerblade.

LICE
love too

Hug Goodbye

I walked off to the changing room thinking about the hug goodbye. I did the 'squeeze release' with her (where you give a final squeeze and let go) rather than the 'pat and out' (where you give them a pat on the back and that signals the letting go). And straight afterwards it was awkward, as though a line had been crossed. I know a few of her male friends have been telling her that they are in love with her at the moment, and so she is understandably suspicious of men, but still… Is the squeeze release wrong to use with friends? Maybe nudists should never hug, I thought as I pulled my trousers back on.

The Breakup

A warm tub of Haagen-Dazs sat on the floor next to the sofa where she slept and a pile of used tissues huddled nearby like scared albino hampsters. I had made a mistake coming over. She was more upset about her boyfriend leaving than I had been expecting and the last thing she needed right now was her friends hitting on her. I pulled a blanket from a drawer and used it to cover her. I knew I had to do the right thing. I would wait until tomorrow before sending the flowers and discrete packet of condoms.

Every Six Seconds

A DJ thinks about decks a chiropractor thinks about necks a Slovakian thinks about Czechs a weightlifter thinks about pecs an optometrist thinks about specs a hiker thinks about treks a diver thinks about shipwrecks a cyclist thinks about spandex a person in the 'there's no toilet roll left in the dispenser, but I might have something in my bag' situation thinks about Kleenex a Russian thinks about Kopeks a Southern American thinks about Tex-Mex an entomologist thinks about insects and I think of you.

Mariana's Trench

My girlfriend doesn't think
I am deep. And that when
Sperm Whales draw a breath and dive,
they hit their heads
on the shallows of a dip,
a minor kink, in the sea floor.

She thinks finer feelings
can't survive, in the low
pressure, but expand and pop
and great ideas (with big teeth
and glowing protuberances)
cannot stay alive,
when visible from ship to shore.

So the next time we go
swimming I stop and sink
far down into my thoughts.
I fall faster still and see
nothing yet, no stamp
of individuality, no glowing

sparks of quartz. And when I think
I must be deep, deep down
with the dregs, I look up -
and see the sun and
my girlfriend's kicking legs.

The Master Storyteller

He sits down at the campfire, and the babble of voices cease as we feel united by the presence of a master storyteller. The bones of his face are thrown into sharp relief by the dancing light of the flames, and a young couple hold hands in tense anticipation. I would not have brought my girlfriend to this event.

'There was this girl, right?' (No-one nods) *'and she went out one night and woke up the next day in a bath of ice, thinking, "Why am I in a bath of ice?" because she only went out to donate a kidney,'* (he pauses and in the dark, someone whimpers,) *'although, now I come to think of it, she went to a party, before donating a kidney, or maybe she was at this party, the night before she woke up in the bath, and they had kidneys in the buffet, which she missed because she was late, but they had ice for drinks, and she drank too much and woke up in the bath,'* (he leans forward, with hollow eyes,) *'but what I'm not telling you is that the buffet kidneys were actually human kidneys,'* (he leans back,) *'which, luckily, as it turned out, was ok because this girl was vegan and wouldn't've had any, but that's not the end of the story, because in actual fact, the kidneys they ate were hers all along.'* Everyone is speechless, and the young couple flee into the night, terrified.

Badly drawn pig

Everyone Has at Least One Book in Them

The doorbell rang and I answered, uncertain what to expect, maybe
he had come to explain what had happened in those dark caves at
each full moon when we were young; I didn't know if it might
reveal him to be the killer and my suspicion was right or if
it was the person in the mirror and my blackouts were
actually covering a darker secret than tame schizo-
phrenia but then he does have a key to the door
so why ring at all, unless it was someone else
who knew that I was hiding here, which
meant I had been hunted up and could
explain the paranoia of the sanction
inspector yesterday when I had
offered to get his suit dry
cleaned but I couldn't
because of the fact
I had mislaid all
of my fingers
the not so
previous
week

It Could Happen to You

A young girl is walking home along a road and it's night-time and it's raining. A car pulls up ahead of her. She opens the door and the driver looks friendly, so she gets in. Her wet clothes dull the leather of the passenger seat and the driver frowns. She says, "Thanks for giving me a lift home" and he says "You're lucky," she says, "Why?" and he says, "You were polite, the last person I gave a lift to was not so polite, so I had to kill them," and she laughs, but he says, "No seriously, their body's still in the boot," and this time she doesn't laugh, but he smiles and they spend the remainder of the drive home in silence. When he pulls up to her house she says, "Cheers dad, try not to be so late picking me up from hockey next time," and waves him goodbye.

The Castle

I

A king was famous among all
For owning a castle that was impregnable
So confident he was of his castle's might
The king let his guards sleep all night

But when a guard one night got up to pee
What – do you think - did he happen to see?
But the enemy - sneaking in and out the gate
In a way the king did not anticipate

The guard rushed back to tell the rest
Who pointed and laughed as tho' he did jest
Frustrated, the guard became so fraught
He ignored them all and went straight to court

The ladies of the court - they spurned his call
And the lords - they took him for a fool
In fact when no-one did anything
He thought 'That's it', I'm going to the king'

Now the king, he knew, wasn't a stupid man
So the guard decided he needed a plan
As he wouldn't be given the time of day
Unless the king was challenged in some way

That clever guard, he announced to all

At nine that night he would be placed outside the wall
But by the time the clock struck quarter to ten
He would be back inside the wall again.
Once inside, he would head to the central square
So that those who disbelieved would see him there.

II

Nine pm arrived and a crowd watched him go
And the guard waved and put on a show
He waited thirty minutes and from memory
Followed the route that was used by the enemy
He rushed though the sleeping castle, a frown on his face
As he went to meet all at the allotted place

You might think he wanted to look them in the eye
And force them all to eat humble pie
But the reason he said he was doing this for
Was to make the castle he loved secure

He had reached the meeting place, and the time was right
But it was empty, except for the darkness of night

He called out for the king, the lords and the rest
When suddenly a thousand arrows thudded into his chest

The king strode out and ordered the body be shown to all
To prove his castle was – truly – impregnable

The guard had no chance, no time to ask why
The instant the arrows hit - the instant he did die.

III

As the guard's head was now rotting on a spike
The king said there was something he'd quite like -
He ordered the castle walls to be made thick
And a deeper moat with some towers of brick

...but added that the changes were purely cosmetic

The story's moral is the thing
But it's not whether the guard was right or the king
The truth is much clearer and it's plain to see:

No-one likes a smart-arse. Seriously...

Five Days Left to Live

Monday

I'm picking up my post and I'm sorting through my letters!

With the time that I have left, you'd have thought I'd be doing something better!

Like phoning up the pope and writing ten bestsellers!

But I'm picking up my post and I'm sorting through my letters!

Tuesday

I'm sorting through my ipod and deleting the crap songs!

With the time that I have left you wouldn't have thought it'd take long!

But I spent the whole day looking, and I only deleted one!

I'm sorting through my ipod and deleting the crap songs!

Wednesday

I'm getting to level three on my video game!

With the time that I've got left, you'd probably not do the same!

As the baddie is a giant squid that shoots balls of flame!

But I'm getting to level three on my video game!

Thursday

I'm drinking the cure that I made this morning!

Now I have lots of time left, I find terminal diseases boring!

I've fixed the problem and now I've got years before me!

As I'm drinking down the cure I made this morning!

Friday

I'm crossing the street and reading the newspaper!

With the time that I have left, you'd have thought I'd have seen that bus!

But I didn't!

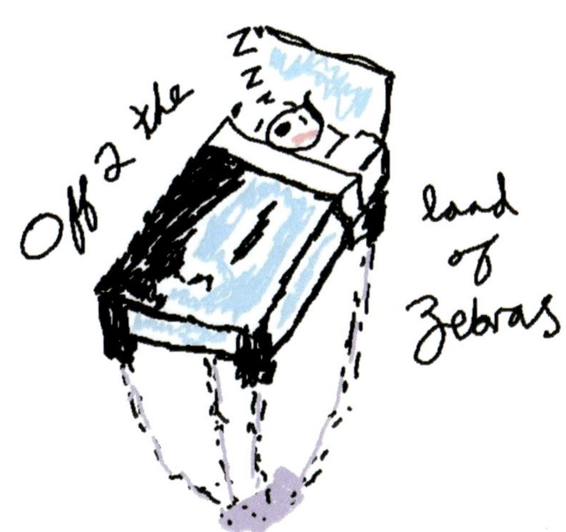

Goodbye

Hello   you've come to the end
you   have seen your friend eat
hope   like it was a hotdog
you   cancelled the weekly jog you
enjoyed   itching your nose
all   the way through this book, yes I saw
the   bogie you secretly ate while watching
crap   on the TV and whispering to the remote;

Luv ya.

thank   the maker of the Tesco ready meal
you   bought from a tramp in exchange for a compliment
and   a whack from his pleasure stick, 'he's no
good!'   your parents say when you bring him round even when you
buy   him a coat to cover him up. But it’s all worth it when he says:

Missing you already snuggleflumps.

she wins

About the Author

Si Stratton is a screenwriter and poet who lives in Cardiff, UK. In 2009 he had two sitcom scripts optioned by Screenplay Productions. He has been published in a Ziv Navoth anthology, and won the Ragged Raven Press prize for his poetry. In August 2009 he released this book of comic poetry for adults. He is currently writing two films; an animated kids' story about headlice and a Christmas story about the first female Santa Claus.

For more info log on to:

www.sistratton.com